The Unknown Region

The Unknown Region

Inspirations on Living and Dying

Edited by
Eileen Campbell

Aquarian/Thorsons
An Imprint of HarperCollinsPublishers

The Aquarian Press
An Imprint of HarperCollins*Publishers*
77–85 Fulham Palace Road,
Hammersmith, London W6 8JB
1160 Battery Street
San Francisco, California 94111–1213

Published by The Aquarian Press 1993
1 3 5 7 9 10 8 6 4 2

A catalogue record for this book
is available from the British Library

ISBN 1 85538 304 7

Printed in Hong Kong by
HarperCollinsManufacturing

Darest thou now O soul,
Walk out with me toward the
 unknown region,
Where neither ground is for the feet
 nor any path to follow?

No map there, nor guide,
Nor voice sounding, nor touch of
 human hand,
Nor face with blooming flesh, nor
 lips, nor eyes, are in that land.

I know it not O soul,
Nor dost thou, all is a blank before us,
All waits undreamed of in that
 region, that inaccessible land.

Till when the ties loosen,
All but the ties eternal, time and space,

Nor darkness, gravitation, sense, nor
  any bounds bounding us.

Then we burst forth, we float,
In time and space O soul, prepared
  for them,
Equal, equipt at last, (O joy! O fruit
  of all!) them to fulfil O soul.

WALT WHITMAN

Introduction

Death is an integral part of life, and yet in our Western culture at the end of the twentieth century we live either denying and evading death or fearing it. Death, the Grim Reaper, is seen as the enemy, standing in the shadows and a stranger to us. We are not taught about death and how to die, though this was not always so, nor indeed is it the case in other cultures where the craft of dying is valued. When confronted, therefore, with death, either directly or indirectly, we are at a loss to know how to handle the experience.

Underlying our fear and avoidance of death is the fear of change. We want everything to stay the same, but nothing ever does, and so it is with us — we are as much in a state of flux as the universe itself. But death is not the end — all the great spiritual traditions of the world have told us so, and it is important that we understand this for it affects our attitude to life. In surrendering to the inevitability of death, we are more able truly to live. We no longer take life for granted and it becomes immensely precious. We also live less selfishly.

Working on this anthology has been immensely rewarding, not at all dark and depressing, as people have felt it might be when I have told them what I have been working on. As with my previous anthologies, I have drawn from a wide range of sources, from the religions of both East and West, from literature and psychology. Beginning with the indivisibility of life and death and the uncertainty of the hour of death, I have organized the anthology loosely in the following sections — fear of death, preparing for and meeting death, grief and mourning, resurrection and immortality, concluding with a section on living life in the knowledge and acceptance of death as a part of life's process.

I have felt inspired and uplifted by these quotations and my hope is that this anthology may be of value not only to those confronting death or bereavement, but also to all those who question life's meaning.

EILEEN CAMPBELL
All Souls Day 1992

It is impossible that anything so natural, so necessary and so universal as death should ever have been designed by Providence as an evil to mankind.

SWIFT

Just as I choose a ship to sail in
or a house to live in,
so I choose a death for my passage
from this life.

SENECA

Death is a huge mystery, but there are two things we can say about it. It is absolutely certain that we will die, and it is uncertain when or how we will die.

SOGYAL RINPOCHE

Lo! as the wind is, so is mortal life:
A moan, a sigh, a sob, a storm.

SIR EDWIN ARNOLD

Death belongs to life as birth does.
The walk is in the raising of the foot
as in the laying of it down.

RABINDRANATH TAGORE

When you are strong and healthy,
You never think of sickness coming,
But it descends with sudden force
Like a stroke of lightning.

When involved in worldly things,
You never think of death's approach;
Quick it comes like thunder
Crashing round your head.

MILAREPA

The life of man on earth, my lord, in comparison with the vast stretches of time about which we know nothing, seems to me to resemble the flight of a sparrow, who enters through a window in the great hall warmed by a blazing fire laid in the centre of it, where you feast with your councillors and liègemen, while outside the tempests and snows of winter rage. And the bird swiftly sweeps through the great hall and goes out the other side, and after this brief respite from winter, he goes back into winter and is lost to your eyes. Such is the brief life of man, of which we know neither what goes before nor what comes after...

VENERABLE BEDE

This existence of ours is as transient as autumn clouds
To watch the birth and death of beings is like looking at the movements of a dance
A lifetime is a flash of lightning in the sky
Rushing by, like a torrent down a steep mountain.

BUDDHA

The world has signed a pact with the devil; it had to ... The terms are clear: if you want to live, you have to die; you cannot have mountains and creeks without space, and space is a beauty married to a blind man. The blind man is Freedom, or Time, and he does not go anywhere without his great dog Death. The world came into being with the signing of the contract.

ANNIE DILLARD

O death, we thank you for the light you cast on our ignorance: you alone convince us of our lowliness, you alone make us know our dignity ... All things summon us to death: nature, almost envious of the good she has given us, tells us often and gives us notice that she cannot for long allow us that scrap of matter she has lent ... she has need of it for other forms, she claims it back for other works.

JACQUES-BÉNIGNE BOSSUET

All mankind is of one author, and is one volume; when one man dies, one chapter is not torn out of the book, but translated into a better language; and every chapter must be so translated; God employs several translators; some pieces are translated by age, some by sickness, some by war, some by justice; but God's hand is in every translation, and his hand shall bind up all our scattered leaves again for that library where every book shall lie open to one another.

JOHN DONNE

For certain is the death of all that is born, certain is the birth of all that dies; therefore, with regard to what is inevitable, you have no reason to grieve.

Bhagavad Gita

*As for man, his days are as grass: as a
    flower of the field, so he flourisheth.
For the wind passeth over it, and it is
    gone; and the place thereof shall
    know it no more.
But the mercy of the Lord is from
    everlasting to everlasting upon
    them that fear him, and his
    righteousness unto children's
    children.*

Psalm 103:15–17

Death, what are you?
— I am the shadow of life.
Death, of what are you born?
— I am born of ignorance.
Death, where is your abode?
— My abode is in the mind of illusion.
Death, do you ever die?
— Yes, when pierced by the arrow of
   the seer's glance.
Death, whom do you draw near to
   you?
— I draw him closer who is attracted
   to me.
Death, whom do you love?
— I love him who longs for me.

Death, whom do you attend?
— I readily attend him who calls on
  me.
Death, whom do you frighten?
— I frighten the one who is not
  familiar with me.
Death, whom do you caress?
— The one who lies trustfully in my
  arms.
Death, with whom are you severe?
— I am severe with him who does not
  readily respond to my call.
Death, whom do you serve?
— I serve the godly, and when he
  returns home I carry his baggage.

HAZRAT INAYAT KHAN

You see, we are all dying. It's only a matter of time. Some of us just die sooner than others.

DUDJOM RINPOCHE

Morning glory
even though you wither
dawn will break anew.

GENGEN'ICHI

All goes onward and outward,
Nothing collapses
And to die is different from
What anyone supposes
And luckier.

WALT WHITMAN

Consider a burning candle: its life is also its death; death and life constantly interact. Just as one cannot experience true joy without having suffered great pain, so life is impossible without death, for they are a single process. Death is life in another form.

PHILIP KAPLEAU

There is a Sufi story about a man who was walking in the market place one afternoon when someone tugged at his sleeve. 'I am Death,' said the figure. 'I just came to warn you that we have an appointment at six o'clock tomorrow morning.' The man was very scared, but he thought he would make good use of the advance information. Cashing in his shares, he bought the three finest, fastest horses in the town, and packing just a towel and a few valuables, he set off across the desert to a distant town where he hoped Death would not be able to find him. All night he rode like the wind, exhausting one horse after the other, until, as six o'clock approached, he came to a small oasis where he *dismounted for a quick drink before continuing. As he walked over to the well, the figure who had been sitting quietly beside it looked at his watch and stood up, saying, 'It's remarkable. I really didn't think you were going to be able to make it!'*

GUY CLAXTON

Do not seek death. Death will find you. But seek the road which makes death a fulfilment.

DAG HAMMARSKJÖLD

What is death? It is a resting from the vibrations of sensation, and the swaying of desire, a stop upon the rambling of thought, and a release from the drudgery about your body.

MARCUS AURELIUS

*The boast of heraldry, the pomp of
    pow'r,
And all that beauty, all that wealth
    e'er gave,
Await alike th' inevitable hour:
The paths of glory lead but to the
    grave.*

THOMAS GRAY

Since time began
the dead alone know peace.
Life is but melting snow.

NANDAI

Do not grieve. Misfortunes will happen to the wisest and best of men. Death will come, always out of season. It is the command of the Great Spirit, and all nations and people must obey. What is past and what cannot be prevented should not be grieved for ... Misfortunes do not flourish particularly in our lives — they grow everywhere.

BIG ELK
Omaha Chief

The conditions bringing death are
    many,
The forces sustaining life are slender
And even these can cause death.
Therefore constantly practise Dharma.

NAGARJUNA

No man should be afraid to die, who hath understood what it is to live.

THOMAS FULLER

To fear death, gentlemen, is nothing other than to think oneself wise when one is not; for it is to think one knows what one does not know. No man knows whether death may not even turn out to be the greatest of blessings for a human being; and yet people fear it as if they knew for certain that it is the greatest of evils.

SOCRATES

Ay, but to die, and go we know not
    where,
To lie in cold obstruction and to rot;
This sensible warm motion to become
A kneaded clod; and the delighted
    spirit
To bathe in fiery floods, or to reside
In thrilling region of thick-ribbed ice,
To be imprisoned in the viewless
    winds
And blown with restless violence
    round about
The pendant world; or to be worse
    than worst
Of those that lawless and incertain
    thoughts

Imagine howling: 'tis too horrible!
The weariest and most loathèd
    worldly life
That age, ache, penury, and
    imprisonment
Can lay on nature, is a paradise
To what we fear of death.

WILLIAM SHAKESPEARE
Measure for Measure III.i.

To conquer illusion and hope, without being overcome by terror: this has been the whole endeavor of my life these past twenty years; to look straight into the abyss without bursting into tears, without begging or threatening, calmly, serenely, preserving the dignity of man; to see the abyss and work as though I were immortal...

NIKOS KAZANTZAKIS

It is my conviction that an intense love of life is the best and perhaps only effective antidote against the fear of death.

IGNACE LEPP

The fear of death
is the fear of letting go.
As it is in life,
so it is in death.
The process of dying
is always a joyous one
once the human fear has been
overcome.

Emmanuel's Book

The brave man is not he who feels no
    fear,
For that were stupid and irrational;
But he, whose noble soul its fear
    subdues,
And bravely shares the danger
    nature shrinks from.

JOANNA BAILLIE

Perhaps the best cure for the fear of death is to reflect that life has a beginning as well as an end. There was a time when we were not: this gives us no concern — why then should it trouble us that a time will come when we shall cease to be? ... To die is only to be as we were before we were born; yet no one feels any remorse or regret, or repugnance, in contemplating this last idea. It is rather a relief and disburthening of the mind: it seems to have been a holiday-time with us then: we were not called to appear upon the stage of life, to wear robes or tatters, to laugh or cry, be hooted or applauded; we had lain **perdus** *all this while, snug, out of harm's way; and had slept out* *our thousands of centuries without wanting to be waked up; at peace and free from care, in a long nonage, in a sleep deeper and calmer than that of infancy, wrapped in the finest and softest dust. And the worst that we dread is, after a short, fretful, feverish being, after vain hopes, and idle fears, to sink to final repose again, and forget the troubled dream of life!*

WILLIAM HAZLITT

But for your Terror
    Where would be Valour?
What is Love for
    But to stand in your way?
Taker and Giver,
For all your endeavour
You leave us with more
    Than you touch with decay!

OLIVER ST JOHN GOGARTY

Heroism is the brilliant triumph of the soul over the flesh — that is to say, over fear ... Heroism is the dazzling and brilliant concentration of courage.

HENRI-FRÉDERIC AMIEL

Mastery of our fear of death enables us to admit that we will die, which then gives us the opportunity for making our lives more meaningful **now**. *Expecting that we will die, we cannot as easily take life for granted or put off living until some unsure future. We are more apt to take action and live our lives fully.*

JUDY TATELBAUM

You have to learn to do everything,
even to die.

GERTRUDE STEIN

*Get used to dying
before death arrives,
for the dead can only live
and the living can only die.*

Old Mexican refrain

When the light of true knowledge has dispelled the darkness of ignorance, when all existence has been seen as without substance, peace ensues when life draws to an end, which seems to cure a long illness at last. Everything, whether stationary or movable, is bound to perish in the end. Be ye therefore mindful and vigilant.

BUDDHACARITA XXVI.88ff.

It is uncertain where death looks for us; let us expect her everywhere: the premeditation of death is a forethinking of liberty. He who hath learned to die, hath unlearned to serve. There is no evil in life, for him that hath well conceived, how the privation of life is no evil. To know how to die doth free us from all subjection and constraint.

MICHEL DE MONTAIGNE

*Sleep with the remembrance of death,
and rise with the thought that you
will not live long.*

UWAIS EL'QARNI

Remember, friends, as you pass by,
as you are now, so once was I,
As I am now, so you must be,
Prepare yourself to follow me.

From a headstone in Ashby, Massachusetts

Death never takes the wise man by surprise.
He is always ready to go.

JOHN DE LA FONTAINE

Those who rightly love wisdom are practising dying, and death to them is the least terrible thing in the world.

SOCRATES

You must prepare yourself for the transition in which there will be none of the things to which you have accustomed yourself. After death your identity will have to respond to stimuli of which you have a chance to get a foretaste here. If you remain attached to the few things with which you are familiar, it will only make you miserable.

EL-GHAZALI

In short, mankind are poor transitory things! They are one day in the rudiments of life, and almost the next turned to mummy or ashes. Your way is therefore to manage this minute in harmony with nature, and part with it cheerfully; and like a ripe olive when you drop, be sure to speak well of the mother that bare you, and make your acknowledgements to the tree that produced you.

MARCUS AURELIUS

*God has fixed the time for my death.
I do not concern myself about that,
but to be always ready, no matter
when it may overtake me. That is the
way all men should live, and then all
would be equally brave.*

STONEWALL JACKSON

To die clinging to nothing means you have realized that nothing is really ours, neither body nor mind nor life itself — and that therefore death is a letting go of that which we never really owned in the first place.

PHILIP KAPLEAU

Death, thy servant, is at my door. He has crossed the unknown sea and brought thy call to my home.

The night is dark and my heart is fearful — yet I will take up the lamp, open my gates and bow to him my welcome. It is thy messenger who stands at my door.

I will worship him with folded hands, and with tears. I will worship him placing at his feet the treasure of my heart.

He will go back with his errand done, leaving a dark shadow on my morning; and in my desolate home only my forlorn self will remain as my last offering to thee.

RABINDRANATH TAGORE

If we will but be still and listen, I think we shall hear these sad trials talking to us: saying, as it were, 'You have known life and enjoyed it, you have tried it and suffered from it; your tent has been pitched in pleasant places among those of dear relations and tried friends, and now they are disappearing from around you. The stakes are loosened one by one, and the canvas is torn away, with no vestige left behind, and you want something which will not be taken away. You want something large enough to fill your heart, and imperishable enough to make it immortal like itself. That something is God.'

SAMUEL PALMER

Not as the world giveth, givest Thou,
O Lover of Souls. What Thou gavest,
Thou takest not away: for what is
Thine is ours always, if we are Thine.
And Life is eternal and love is
immortal, and death is only a
horizon, and a horizon is nothing
save the limit of our sight.

WILLIAM PENN

Death is a friend, not an enemy. It brings to a close all that can be done in this lifetime. If there is unfinished business one can rest assured it will be resolved, either after death or in the next life.

Z'EV BEN SHIMON HALEVI

So live that when thy summons comes
To join the innumerable caravan
Which moves to that mysterious realm
Where each shall take his chamber
In the silent halls of death
Thou go not like the quarry slave at
    night
Scourged to his dungeon
But sustained and soothed by an
    unfaltering trust.
Approach thy grave like one
Who wraps the drapery of his couch
    about him
And lies down to pleasant dreams.

WILLIAM CULLEN BRYANT

Just as a well spent day brings happy sleep,
so a life well used brings happy death.

LEONARDO DA VINCI

A dignified, or 'good' death is one in which there is no railing or struggling against imminent death — above all, a death without sadness, without regret, without apprehension, without bitterness, without terror. It is dying freely, naturally, like falling asleep, not clinging to or clutching at life, just 'going with the flow' — not 'flow' or 'letting go' in a psychological sense, but in the transcendent sense of the 'eternal yea', of yielding to an inner, mysterious force that takes over when all self-striving ceases.

PHILIP KAPLEAU

A good death
does honour to a whole life.

PETRARCH

Rouse thee, my fainting soul, and
    play the man;
And thro' such warring span
Of life and thought as still has to be
    trod,
Prepare to meet thy God.
And while the storm of that
    bewilderment
Is for a season spent,
And, ere afresh the ruin on me fall,
Use well the interval.

CARDINAL NEWMAN

To die artfully is to die thinking of nothing, wishing for nothing, wanting to understand nothing, clinging to nothing — just fading away like clouds in the sky. That is the acme of artful dying; such an accomplishment, though, presupposes considerable spiritual insight. To be able to die thinking of nothing implies that through meditation and other spiritual practices, you have gained control over your wayward thoughts and a high degree of mastery over your emotions. To die wishing for nothing assumes you have realized that fundamentally you are whole and complete and therefore lack nothing. To die wanting to understand nothing means you have perceived that all things, including your thoughts, feelings and perceptions, are impermanent, arising when certain causes and conditions bring them into being and passing away with the emergence of new causal factors.

PHILIP KAPLEAU

*I have got my leave. Bid me farewell,
my brothers! I bow to you all and take
my departure.*

*Here I give back the keys of my door
— and I give up all claims to my
house. I only ask for last kind words
from you.*

*We were neighbours for long, but I
received more than I could give. Now
the day has dawned and the lamp
that lit my dark corner is out. A
summons has come and I am ready
for my journey.*

RABINDRANATH TAGORE

For I know that my redeemer liveth,
*   and that he shall stand at the*
*   latter day upon the earth.*
And though after my skin worms
*   destroy this body, yet in my flesh*
*   shall I see God.*

Job 19:25–6

I know the truth — give up all other truths! No need for people everywhere on earth to struggle. Look — it is evening, look, it is nearly night: what do you speak of, poets, lovers, generals? The wind is level now, the earth is wet with dew, the storm of stars in the sky will turn to quiet. And soon all of us will sleep under the earth, we who never let each other sleep above it.

MARINA TSVETAYEVA

Yea, though I walk through the valley of the shadow of death, I will fear no evil: for thou art with me; thy rod and thy staff they comfort me.

Psalm 23:4

Because I could not stop for Death —
He kindly stopped for me —
The Carriage held but just
      Ourselves —
And Immortality.

We slowly drove — He knew no haste
And I had put away
My labor and my leisure too,
For this Civility —

We passed the School, where Children
      strove
At Recess — in the Ring —
We passed the Fields of Gazing
      Grain —
We passed the Setting Sun —

Or rather — He passed Us —
The Dews drew quivering and chill —
For only Gossamer, my Gown —
My Tippet — only Tulle —

We paused before a House that seemed
A Swelling of the Ground —
The Roof was scarcely visible —
The Cornice — in the Ground —

Since then — 'tis Centuries — and
  yet
Feels shorter than the Day
I first surmised the Horses' Heads
Were toward Eternity —

EMILY DICKINSON

In the night of death hope sees a star and
listening love can hear the rustle of a wing.

ROBERT INGERSOLL

Rain clouds clear away:
above the lotus shines
the perfect moon.

SEISHU

*On the day when death will knock at
   thy door
What will thou offer him?
I will set before my guest the full vessel
   of my life.
I will never let him go with empty
   hands...*

RABINDRANATH TAGORE

For what is to die but to stand naked in the wind and to melt into the sun? And what is it to cease breathing, but to free the breath from its restless tides, that it may rise and expand and seek God unencumbered?

KHALIL GIBRAN

Abide with me; fast falls the eventide;
The darkness deepens; Lord,
with me abide;
When other helpers fail, and comforts
flee,
Help of the helpless, O, abide
with me.

HENRY FRANCIS LYTE

When I die
what I shall see will be
the lustrous moon

HAYAKURI

When the time comes for dying will the heart be light and free?

If there is fear for the future the heart will be frightened, like a sheep suddenly penned alone for dipping or shearing or slaughter, with legs taut and startled eyes, fearing its fate and unable to escape.

If there is remorse for the past, the heart will be heavy and will drag its feet, like a puppy brought to a puddle of its making, only fearing punishment.

If there is attachment to the things of the world, the heart will be grounded, as a wasp on a honey-pot, wings buzzing noisily, but feet sweetly stuck where they want to belong.

If there is longing for something imagined, the heart will plunge like a pig every way but where the gate is open.

The heart will be light and free if the man has already come to the true worship of God.

Then the soul is liberated before the call of death.

Then the heart, having already tasted of purification, rejoices with the soul.

And the soul herself slips away from the body gently, almost imperceptibly, like a host slipping away from a party before his guests, unnoticed until he is gone.

For the liberated soul, death is easy, quiet, gentle.

Those who know the sweetness of submission to God will understand that the last submission in this world may be sweet indeed, being too the first submission in the next.

All who come to the true worship of God, however recent is their coming, however incomplete their submission, however early the stage of their purification, can be peaceful in the sure prospect of a gentle passage of the soul out of this body and on into life.

HUBERT VON BISSING

Rest and peace external give them,
Lord Our God; and light for
evermore shine down upon them.

VERDI

*Dawn breaks
and blossoms open
gates of paradise.*

SAIMU

The tomb is not a blind alley; it is a thoroughfare.
It closes on the twilight. It opens on the dawn.

VICTOR HUGO

*Death is merely the other side of life;
it is familiar, intimately known by
every one of us in its benignant
essence. No one at the moment of
dying fears death; most welcome it.
To all, it is the most natural thing in
the world. The sad thing at the
moment of dying is that the living do
not understand.*

BARRY LONG

For I am persuaded, that neither death, nor life, nor angels, nor principalities, nor powers, nor things present, nor things to come, nor height, nor depth, nor any other creature shall be able to separate us from the love of God which is in Christ Jesus our Lord.

Romans 8:38–9

Grief is itself a medicine.

WILLIAM COWPER

*Blessed are they that mourn: for they
shall be comforted.*

Matthew 5:4

Grief has a quality of healing in it that is very deep because we are forced to a depth of emotion that is usually below the threshold of our awareness.

STEPHEN LEVINE

Great grief ... transforms the wretched.

VICTOR HUGO

Loss is life's non-negotiable side. It is the time when we learn, unconditionally, that we are powerless over things we thought we had a grip on. But it doesn't stop there, because every ending brings a new beginning. Loss is often a blessing in disguise.

STEPHANIE ERICSSON

And you would accept the seasons of
*   your heart,*
even as you have always accepted the
*   seasons*
that pass over your fields.
And you would watch with serenity
through the winters of your grief.

KHALIL GIBRAN

And you must be able to bear your sorrow; even if it seems to crush you, you will be able to stand up again, for human beings are so strong, and your sorrow must become an integral part of yourself; you mustn't run away from it.

Do not relieve your feeling through hatred ... Give your sorrow all the space and shelter in yourself that is its due, for if everyone bears grief honestly and courageously, the sorrow that now fills the world will abate...

ETTE HILLESUM

When pain is to be borne, a little courage helps more than much knowledge, a little human sympathy more than much courage, and the least tincture of the love of God more than all.

C. S. LEWIS

Happiness is beneficial to the body,
but it is grief that develops the powers
of the mind.

MARCEL PROUST

The terrible fire of grief is an energetic furnace, refining character, personality, intellect, and soul. It is a catalyst for creation. What is created may be dreadful — a distorted, unapproachable monument to despair — or a distillation of experience that is wholesome, useful, bright, and even wise.

PEG ELLIOT MAYO

Grief discriminates against no one. It kills. Maims. And cripples. It is the ashes from which the phoenix rises, and the mettle of re-birth. It returns life to the living dead. It teaches that there is nothing absolutely true, or untrue. It assures the living that we know nothing for certain. It humbles. It shrouds. It blackens. It enlightens.

Grief will make a new person out of you, if it doesn't kill you in the making.

STEPHANIE ERICSSON

Mourning is a time of new mastery over ourselves and our lives. Recovery comes in the days ahead, when mourning is completed and a new balance is found.

JUDY TATELBAUM

When I am dead, my dearest,
    Sing no sad songs for me;
Plant thou no roses at my head
    Nor shady cypress tree:
Be the green grass above me
    With showers and dewdrops
  wet;
And if thou wilt, remember.
    And if thou wilt, forget.
I shall not see the shadows,
    I shall not feel the rain;
I shall not hear the nightingale
    Sing on, as if in pain;
And dreaming through the twilight
    That doth not rise nor set,
Haply I may remember,
    And haply may forget.

CHRISTINA ROSSETTI

Do not stand at my grave and weep;
I am not there. I do not sleep.
I am a thousand winds that blow.
I am the diamond glints on snow.
I am the sunlight on ripened grain.
I am the gentle autumn's rain.
When you awaken in the morning's
    hush,
I am the swift uplifting rush
Of quiet birds in circled flight.
I am the soft stars that shine at night.
Do not stand at my grave and cry;
I am not there. I did not die.

ANON

And God shall wipe away all tears from their eyes; and there shall be no more death, neither sorrow, nor crying, neither shall there be any more pain: for the former things are passed away.

Revelation 21:4

They shall not grow old, as we that
*   are left grow old:*
Age shall not weary them nor the
*   years condemn.*
At the going down of the sun, and in
*   the morning,*
We will remember them.

LAURENCE BINYON

Be careful, then, and be gentle about
    death.
For it is hard to die, it is difficult to
    go through
the door, even when it opens.

And the poor dead, when they have
    left the walled
and silvery city of the now hopeless
    body
where are they to go, Oh where are
    they to go?

They linger in the shadow of the
    earth.
The earth's long conical shadow is
    full of souls
that cannot find a way across the sea
    of change.

Be kind, Oh be kind to your dead
and give them a little encouragement
and help them to build their little
   ship of death.

For the soul has a long, long journey
   after death
to the sweet home of pure oblivion.
Each needs a little ship, a little ship
and the proper store of meal for the
   longest journey.

Oh, from out of your heart
provide for your dead once more,
   equip them
like departing mariners, lovingly.

D. H. LAWRENCE

It is by learning to live through and to understand the death of others, in them and in ourselves, that we can best learn to face death and eventually face our own death...

METROPOLITAN ANTHONY

Love is not changed by Death,
And nothing is lost and all in the
end is harvest.

EDITH SITWELL

Everything in nature is resurrection.

VOLTAIRE

*Like last year's vegetation our
human life but dies down to its root
and still puts forth its green blade
into eternity.*

HENRY DAVID THOREAU

Verily, verily, I say unto you, Except a corn of wheat fall into the ground and die, it abideth alone; but if it die, it bringeth forth much fruit.

John 12:24

Either death is a state of nothingness and utter unconsciousness, or, as men say, there is a change and migration of the soul from this world to another. Now if death be of such a nature, I say that to die is to gain; for eternity is then only a single night.

PLATO

Then death, so call'd, is but old
  matter dress'd
In some new figure, and a varied
  vest.
Thus all things are but alter'd,
  nothing dies;
And here and there the unbodied
  spirit flies...
From tenement to tenement though
  toss'd,
The soul is still the same, the figure
  only lost:
And, as the soften'd wax new seals
  receives,
This face assumes, and that
  impression leaves;
Now call'd by one, now by another
  name,

The Form is only changed, the wax is
    still the same.
So death, so call'd, can but the form
    deface;
The immortal soul flies out in empty
    space,
To seek her fortune in some other
    place.

OVID

Total annihilation is impossible. We are the prisoners of an infinity without outlet, wherein nothing perishes, wherein everything is dispersed, but nothing lost. Neither a body nor a thought can drop out of the universe, out of time and space. Not an atom of our flesh, not a quiver of our nerves, will go where they cease to be, for there is no place where anything ceases to be. The brightness of a star extinguished millions of years ago still wanders in the ether where our eyes will perhaps behold it this very night, pursuing its endless road. It is the same with all that we see, as with all that we do not see.

MAURICE MAETERLINCK

I am the resurrection and the life: he
   that believeth in me, though he
   were dead, yet shall he live:
And whosoever liveth and believeth in
   me shall never die...

John 11:25–6

There is no death of anything save in appearance. That which passes over from essence to nature seem to be birth, and what passes over from nature to essence seems to be death. Nothing really is originated, and nothing ever perishes; but only now comes into sight and now vanishes. It appears by reason of the density of matter, and disappears by reason of the tenuity of essence. But it is always the same, differing only in motion and condition.

APOLLONIUS OF TYANA

Every new born being indeed comes fresh and blithe into the new existence, and enjoys it as a free gift: but there is and can be, nothing freely given. Its fresh existence is paid for by the old age and death of a worn-out existence which has perished, but which contained the indestructible seed out of which this new existence has arisen: they are one being.

ARTHUR SCHOPENHAUER

We commonly know that we are going to die, though we do not know that we are going to be born. But are we sure this is so? We may have had the most gloomy forebodings on this head and forgotten all about them.

Death is the dissolving of a partnership, the partners to which survive and go elsewhere. It is the corruption or breaking up of that society which we have called Ourself. The corporation is at an end, both its soul and body cease as a whole, but the immortal constituents do not cease and never will.

*I must have it that neither are the good rewarded not the bad punished in a future state, but everyone must start anew quite irrespective of anything they have done here, and must try his luck again, and go on trying it again and again **ad infinitum**. Some of our lives, then, will be lucky and some unlucky.*

SAMUEL BUTLER

It is the secret of the world that all things subsist and do not die, but only retire a little from sight and afterwards return again.

RALPH WALDO EMERSON

I am a soul. I know well that what I shall render up to the grave is not myself. That which is myself will go elsewhere. Earth, thou art not my abyss! ... The whole creation is a perpetual ascension, from brute to man, from man to God. To divest ourselves more and more of matter, to be clothed more and more with spirit, such is the law. Each time we die we gain more of life. Souls pass from one sphere to another without loss of personality, become more and more bright.

VICTOR HUGO

I am Yesterday, To-day, and To-morrow, and I have the power to be born a second Time; I am the divine hidden Soul who createth the gods ... I am the Lord of the men who are raised up; the Lord who cometh forth from out of the darkness, and whose forms of existence are of the house wherein are the dead...

The [Egyptian] Book of the Dead LXIV

Tis but as when one layeth
His worn out robes away,
And, taking new ones, sayeth
'These will I wear today!'
So putteth by the Spirit
Lightly its garb of flesh,
And passeth to inherit
A residence afresh...

SIR EDWIN ARNOLD

*I feel my immortality o'er sweep all
    pains,
all tears, all times, all fears; and
    peal,
like the external thunders of the deep,
into my ears this truth — thou livest
    forever.*

GEORGE GORDON, LORD BYRON

We all return; it is this certainty that gives meaning to life and it does not make the slightest difference whether or not in a later incarnation we remember the former life. What counts is not the individual and his comfort, but the great aspiration to the perfect and pure which goes on in each incarnation.

GUSTAV MAHLER

*Death be not proud, though some
    have called thee
Mighty and dreadful, for, thou art
    not so,
For, those, whom thou thinkest, thou
    dost overthrow,
Die not, poor death, nor yet canst
    thou kill me.
From rest and sleep, which but thy
    pictures be,
Much pleasure, then from thee, much
    more must flow,
And soonest our best men with thee
    do go,
Rest of their bones, and soul's delivery
Thou art slave to Fate, Chance,
    kings, and desperate men,
And dost with poison, war, and
    sickness dwell,*

And poppy, or charms can make us
  sleep as well,
And better than thy stroke; why
  swellst thou then?
One short sleep past, we wake
  eternally,
And death shall be no more; death,
  thou shalt die.

JOHN DONNE

*When you commit me to the
grave, say not 'Farewell, farewell!'
For the grave is a veil over the
reunion of paradise.*

*Having seen the going-down,
look upon the coming-up; how should
setting impair the sun and the moon?*

*To you it appears as setting,
but it is a rising; the tomb appears as
a prison, but it is release for the soul.*

*What seed ever went down into
the earth which did not grow?
Why do you doubt so regarding the
human seed?*

JALĀL AL-DĪN RŪMI

The personality disappears at death, but we lose nothing thereby; for it is only the manifestation of quite a different Being — a Being ignorant of Time, and, consequently, knowing neither life nor death ... When we die, we throw off our personality like a worn-out garment, and rejoice because we are about to receive a new and better one...

ARTHUR SCHOPENHAUER

The old always gives way and is replaced by the new, and one thing must be made good out of another. There is no dark pit of Hell awaiting anyone. Matter is needed, so that later generations may grow; yet all of them, too, will follow you when they have lived out their span of life. As with you, generations have passed away before, and will do so again. Thus one thing will never cease to arise from another. To none is life given in freehold; to all on lease. Look back at the eternity of time that passed before we were born, and see how utterly unimportant it is to us. Nature holds this up to us as a mirror of the time that is to come after we are dead. Is there anything

*terrifying in the sight? Anything to
grieve over? Is it not a rest more
tranquil than any sleep?*

LUCRETIUS

Behold, I shew you a mystery; We shall not all sleep, but we shall all be changed,

In a moment, in the twinkling of an eye, at the last trump: for the trumpet shall sound, and the dead shall be raised incorruptible, and we shall be changed.

For this corruptible must put on incorruption, and this mortal must put on immortality.

So when this corruptible shall have put on incorruption, and this mortal shall have put on

*immortality, then shall be brought
to pass the saying that is written,
Death is swallowed up in victory.*

*O Death, where is thy sting?
O grave, where is thy victory?*

*The sting of death is sin; and
the strength of sin is the law.*

*But thanks be to God, which
giveth us the victory through our
Lord Jesus Christ.*

1 Corinthians 15:51–7

And death shall have no dominion.
Dead men naked they shall be one
With the man in the wind and the
    west moon;
When their bones are picked clean
    and the clean bones gone
They shall have stars at elbow and
    foot;
Though they go mad they shall be
    sane,
Though they sink through the sea they
    shall rise again;
Though lovers be lost love shall not;
And death shall have no dominion.

DYLAN THOMAS

Everything goeth, everything returneth; eternally rolleth the wheel of existence.

Everything dieth, everything blossometh forth again; eternally runneth on the year of existence.

Everything breaketh, everything is integrated anew; eternally buildeth itself the same house of existence. All things separate, all things again greet one another; eternally true to itself remaineth the ring of existence. Behold, we know what thou teachest, that all things eternally return, and ourselves with them, and that we have already existed times without number, and all things with us...

FRIEDRICH NIETZSCHE

As a goldsmith, taking a piece of gold, transforms it into another newer and more beautiful form, even so this self, casting off this body and dissolving its ignorance, makes for itself another newer and more beautiful form...

Brhadāranyaka IV:43–4.

Death is like taking off a tight shoe.
Even when you are dead,
you are still alive.
You do not cease to exist at death.
That is only illusion.
You go through the doorway of death
   alive
and there is no altering of the
   consciousness
It is not a strange land you go to
but a land of living reality
where the growth process is a
   continuation.

Emmanuel's Book

A flower blossoms; then withers and dies. It leaves a fragrance behind, which, long after its delicate petals are but a little dust, still lingers in the air ... Let a note be struck on an instrument, and the faintest sound produces an eternal echo. A disturbance is created on the invisible waves of the shoreless ocean of space, and the vibration is never wholly lost. Its energy being once carried from the world of matter into the immaterial world will live for ever. And man, we are asked to believe, man, the living, thinking, reasoning entity, the indwelling deity of our nature's crowning masterpiece, will evacuate his casket and be no more! Would the principle of continuity which exists even for the so-called inorganic matter, for a floating atom, be denied to the spirit, whose attributes are consciousness, memory, mind, LOVE! Really, the very idea is preposterous...

HELENA PETROVNA BLAVATSKY

Your essence was not born and will not die. It is neither being nor nonbeing. It is not a void nor does it have form. It experiences neither pleasure nor pain. If you ponder what it is in you that feels the pain of this sickness, and beyond that you do not think or desire or ask anything, and if your mind dissolves like vapour in the sky, then the path to rebirth is blocked and the moment of instant release has come.

BASSUI

A man acts according to the desires to which he clings. After death he goes to the next world bearing in his mind the subtle impressions of his deeds; and, after reaping there the harvest of those deeds, he returns again to this world of action. Thus he who has desire continues subject to rebirth.

He who lacks discrimination, whose mind is unsteady and whose heart is impure, never reaches the goal, but is born again and again. But he who has discrimination, whose mind is steady and whose heart is pure, reaches the goal and, having reached it, is born no more.

Upanishads

Now our whole life, from birth unto death, with all its dreams, is it not in its turn also a dream, which we take as the real life, the reality of which we do not doubt only because we do not know of the other, more real life? ... The dreams of our present life are the environment in which we work out the impressions, thoughts, feelings of a former life ... As we live through thousands of dreams in our present life, so is our present life only one of many thousands of such lives which we enter from the other, more real life ... and then return after death. Our life is but one of the dreams of that more real life, and so it is endlessly until the very last one, the very real life — the life of God.

LEO TOLSTOY

When the journey of my life has
     reached its end,
and since no relatives go with me
     from this world
I wander in the bardo state alone,
may the peaceful and wrathful
     buddhas send out the power of their
     compassion
and clear away the dense darkness of
     ignorance.

When parted from beloved friends,
     wandering alone,
my own projections' empty forms
     appear,
may the buddhas send out the power
     of their compassion
so that the bardo's terrors do not
     come.

The Tibetan Book of the Dead

God generates beings, and sends them
back over and over again, till they
return to him.

The Koran

It is absolutely necessary that the soul should be healed and purified, and if this does not take place during its life on earth it must be accomplished in future lives.

ST GREGORY

Observe constantly that all things take place by change, and accustom thyself to consider that the nature of the Universe loves nothing so much as to change things which are and to make new things like them. For everything that exists is in a manner the seed of that which will be.

MARCUS AURELIUS

And let us, above all things, never forget that in due course the dead will come back, and we never know when we shall see looking out at us from the eyes of a little child a soul we have known. Let us therefore, making expression for the love that now may have no earthly outlet, turn it to the endeavour of making the world a better place for the return of those we love.

DION FORTUNE

In the last analysis it is our conception of death which decides all our answers to the questions life puts to us.

DAG HAMMARSKJÖLD

Fear not that thy life shall come to an end, but rather fear that it shall never have a beginning.

CARDINAL NEWMAN

The tragedy of life is what dies inside a man while he lives.

ALBERT EINSTEIN

Do not act as if you had ten thousand years to throw away. Death stands at your elbow. Be good for something, while you live and it is in your power.

MARCUS AURELIUS

Be aware of impermanence, because life is short and everything we do counts. Family relationships and friendships are precious beyond measure. If only we could live our life as if each moment were our last — opening and accepting the as-it-is-ness, the nature of reality — we would connect with that essential part of ourselves that does not die. Ask yourself, is my life equipping me for my death? Because you become what you practise. What you are is what you have been. What you will be is what you are now.

CHAGDUD TULKU RINPOCHE

If we accept death as necessity rather than strive to demote it to the level of accident, energies now bound up in continuing strivings to shelve the idea of death will be available to us for more constructive aspects of living, perhaps even fortify our gift for creative splendour against our genius for destruction.

HERMAN FEIFEL

The more we accept death, the more it will be easier for us to discover a true direction in life. Accepting death frees us to live life to its fullest, and to discover a happiness and joy in being alive. If we refuse to accept death, we can only stagger blindly through our lives, with no idea of what we really want or need, or where we are going.

SOGYAL RINPOCHE

Death is the only certainty there is; life itself is uncertain. If you want to be more alive you have to live in uncertainty, you have to move into the unknown. What your life is like is what your death will be like. If you live your life without fear, welcoming the unknown, your death will be without fear. You will embrace death like a bridegroom embracing his beloved.

BHAGWAN SHREE RAJNEESH

I would like to live ... open to time and death painlessly, noticing everything, remembering nothing, choosing the given with a fierce and pointed will.

ANNIE DILLARD

It's easy enough to say that life is a process. Yet, how many of us live our life as if it is a product? When we get or have what we want: a better job, a new place to live, thinner, smarter, older (younger?), serenity, peace, etc. etc., then we'll really have something. Then our lives will be worth living. The only known destination in life is death, and even dying is a process.

JAN JOHNSON DRANTELL

There would be no chance to get to know death at all if it happened only once. But unfortunately life is nothing but a continuing dance of birth and death, a dance of changes.

These changes, these small deaths, which happen so often and dominate our lives, are our living links with death. They are death's pulses, death's heartbeats, prompting us to let go more and more of all the things we cling to, inviting us to become wiser, kinder and more generous.

Let us then work with these changes now, in life: that is the real way to prepare for death.

SOGYAL RINPOCHE

There is no need to be afraid of death. It is not the end of the physical body that should worry us. Rather, our concern must be to live while we're alive — to release our inner selves from the spiritual death that comes with living behind a facade designed to conform to external definitions of who and what we are. Every individual human being born on this earth has the capacity to become a unique and special person unlike any who has ever existed before or will ever exist again.

ELISABETH KÜBLER-ROSS

I want to be thoroughly used up when I die ... Life is no brief candle to me. It's a sort of splendid torch which I've got to hold up for the moment and I want to make it burn as brightly as possible before handing it on to future generations.

GEORGE BERNARD SHAW

Rise up, why mourn this transient
  world of men?
Pass your whole life in gratitude and
  joy.
Had humankind been freed from
  womb and tomb,
When would your turn have come to
  live and love?

OMAR KHAYYAM

*Learn to die and thou shalt live,
for there shall none learn to live
that hath not learned to die.*

The Book of the Craft of Dying

Having the courage to confront death with honesty inevitably means that we examine our lives, our values, our ideas, and our sense of meaning, so that eventually we can create an existence that has satisfaction and purpose. By accepting death as a natural life process, we can live our lives with more zest and depth, and we can achieve the greatest richness possible. In other words, the courage to accept death will enhance our lives.

JUDY TATELBAUM

To be reborn hourly and daily in this life, we need to die — to give of ourselves wholly to the demands of the moment, so that we utterly 'disappear'. Thoughts of past, present, or future, of life and death, of this world and the next, are transcended in the superabundance of the now. Time and timelessness coalesce: this is the moment of eternity. Thus our every act is a matter either of giving life or taking it away. If we perform each act with total absorption, we give life to our life. If we do things half-heartedly, we kill that life.

PHILIP KAPLEAU

You are surrounded by gifts
every living moment of every day.
Let yourself feel appreciation for their
presence in your life
and take the time
to acknowledge
their splendor.

LON G. NUNGESSER

*The acknowledgment of
impermanence holds
within it the key to life itself.*

STEPHEN LEVINE

*If I were certain that death was no more than a sleep, from which I should assuredly awaken to another phase of existence — I know well enough what I would do ... I would live a different life **now** ... so that when the new Future dawned for me, I might not be haunted or tortured by the remembrance of a misspent past!*

MARY MACKAY

What I know of such things [the dying and the dead] explains why I don't waste much lifetime mowing grass or washing cars or making beds or shining shoes or washing dishes. It explains why I don't honk at people who are slow to move at green lights. And why I don't kill spiders. There isn't time or need for all this.

ROBERT FULGHUM

Life becomes immense when we start recognizing that there is no assurance that we will live out this day. Our fantasies and presumptions that we will live forever confuse us as we enter death. In reality, all the time we have is right now. The past and the future are dreams. Only this moment is real. If we come newborn to each moment, we will experience life directly, not dream it.

STEPHEN LEVINE

Tell me not, in mournful numbers,
Life is but an empty dream! —
For the soul is dead that slumbers,
And things are not what they seem.
Life is real! Life is earnest!
And the grave is not its goal,
Dust thou art, to dust returneth,
Was not spoken of the soul...

HENRY WADSWORTH LONGFELLOW

*If we really want to live, we'd better
start at once to try.*

W. H. AUDEN

For none of us liveth to himself, and no man dieth to himself.
For whether we live, we live unto the Lord;
and whether we die, we die unto the Lord:
whether we live therefore, or die, we are the Lord's.

Romans 14:7–8

When you die and go to heaven our Maker is not going to ask, 'Why didn't you discover the cure for such and such? Why didn't you become the Messiah?' The only question we will be asked in that precious moment is 'Why didn't you become you?'

ELIE WIESEL

One of the most important feelings to have is a satisfaction with life. Those who appreciate the value their life has to themselves and to others, enjoy life more. Recognizing that your life has meaning and that you make a difference can help lessen your anxiety about death.

LON G. NUNGESSER

You would know the secret of death.
But how shall you find it unless you
seek it in the heart of life?
The owl whose night-bound eyes are
blind unto the day cannot unveil
the mystery of light.
If you would indeed behold the spirit
of death, open your heart wide
unto the body of life.
For life and death are one, even as
the river and sea are one.

KHALIL GIBRAN

Live all you can; it's a mistake not to. It doesn't so much matter what you do in particular, so long as you have your life. If you haven't had that, what have you had?

HENRY JAMES

He who dies
Before he dies
Does not die
When he dies

ABRAHAM A SANCTA CLARA

Death is a very positive force because it tells me I have limited time. No one will get out of this world alive. But there are some of us who actually believe we will. We act as if we have forever! 'I've always wanted to climb a mountain ... I'll do it tomorrow.' You may not.

LEO BUSCAGLIA

*There is only one courage and that is
the courage to go on dying to the past,
not to collect it, not to accumulate it,
not to cling to it. We all cling to the
past, and because we cling to the past
we become unavailable to the present.*

BHAGWAN SHREE RAJNEESH

If I had my life to live over...
I'd dare to make more mistakes next
   time.
I'd relax. I would limber up.
I would be sillier than I have been
   this trip.
I would take fewer things seriously. I
   would take more chances.
I would take more trips.
I would climb more mountains and
   swim more rivers.
I would eat more ice cream and less
   beans.
I would perhaps have more actual
   troubles,
But I'd have fewer imaginary ones.

NADINE STAIR

The knowledge that we must die gives us our perspective for living, our sense of finitude, our conviction of the value of every moment, our determination to live in such a fashion that we transcend our tragic limitation.

JOHN McMANNERS

When you accept that you're going to die, you kid yourself a little less. Priorities change; you look at life differently. When you begin to reflect on death, you begin to live. It is part of the process of growing up.

ALLEGRA TAYLOR

Death can show us the way, for when we know and understand completely that our time on this earth is limited, and that we have no way of knowing when it will be over, then we must live each day as if it were the only one we had.

ELISABETH KÜBLER-ROSS

The more you open to life, the less death becomes the enemy. When you start using death as a means of focusing on life, then everything becomes just as it is, just this moment, an extraordinary opportunity to be really alive.

STEPHEN LEVINE

Life is either a daring adventure or nothing.

HELEN KELLER

Acknowledgements and Further Reading

The editor would like to thank the following authors and publishers for permission to reprint material from their books:

Budge, E. A.Wallis, *The Book of the Dead* (Arkana, 1985).

Enright, D. J., *The Oxford Book of Death* (Oxford University Press, 1983).

Ericsson, Stephanie, *Companion Through the Darkness: Inner Dialogues on Grief* (HarperCollins Inc. & The Aquarian Press, 1993).

Feinstein, David & Elliot Mayo, Peg, *Rituals for Living and Dying: How We Can Turn Loss and the Fear of Death into an Affirmation of Life* (HarperSanFrancisco, 1990).

Fremantle, Francesca & Trungpa, Chögyam, *The Tibetan Book of the Dead: The Great Liberation Through Hearing in the Bardo* (Shambhala, 1975).

Gibran, Khalil, *The Prophet* (Knopf, 1961).

Head, Joseph & Cranston, S.L. (eds), *Reincarnation: An East-West Anthology* (Theosophical Publishing House, 1961).

Hoffman, Yoel (ed.), *Japanese Death Poems — Written by Zen Monks and Haiku Poets on the Verge of Death* (Charles E.Tuttle Company, 1986).

Idries, Shah, *The Way of the Sufi* (Penguin Books, 1974).

Kapleau, Philip, *The Wheel of Life and Death: A Practical and Spiritual Guide* (Doubleday, 1989).

Kübler-Ross, Elisabeth, *On Death and Dying: What the dying have to teach doctors, nurses, clergy and their own families* (Macmillan, 1969).

— Death: *The Final Stage of Growth* (Simon & Schuster, 1986).

Levine, Stephen, *Who Dies? An Investigation of Conscious Living and Conscious Dying* (Anchor Books, Doubleday, 1982).

Lewis, C. S., *A Grief Observed* (Faber, 1992).

Mullen, Peter, *Death Be Not Proud* (Fount, HarperCollins, 1989).

Nungesser, Lon G., *How to Live Until You Say Goodbye: Axioms for Survivors* (HarperSanFrancisco, 1992).

Rodegast, Pat & Stanton, Judith, *Emmanuel's Book: A manual for living comfortably in the cosmos* (Bantam, 1985).

Sogyal Rinpoche, *The Tibetan Way of Living and Dying* (HarperSanFrancisco & Rider, 1992).

Tatelbaum, Judy, *The Courage to Grieve: Creative Living, Recovery and Growth Through Grief* (Harper & Row, 1980).

Taylor, Allegra, *Acquainted with the Night: A Year on the Frontiers of Death* (Fontana/Collins, 1989).